ideals®
SWEETHEART

Sweet! Ah, sweet are the hours
We spend in Sweetheart days,
Filling our hearts overflowing
With love that will last always.

Love that will conquer trouble
And dry away the tears,
Love that will rule and master
Our lives throughout the years.

Christopher Thomas Haley

ISBN 0-8249-1040-0

Publisher, Patricia A. Pingry
Editors/Ideals, Dorothy L. Gibbs
Ramona Richards
Managing Editor, Marybeth Owens
Art Director, Jennifer Rundberg
Staff Artist, David Lenz
Permissions, Kathleen Gilbert
Copy Editor, Susan DuBois

IDEALS–Vol. 43, No. 1 February MCMLXXXVI IDEALS (ISSN 0019-137X) is published eight times a year,
February, March, May, June, August, September, November, December
by IDEALS PUBLISHING CORPORATION, Nelson Place at Elm Hill Pike, Nashville, Tenn. 37214
Second class postage paid at Nashville, Tennessee, and additional mailing offices.
Copyright © MCMLXXXVI by IDEALS PUBLISHING CORPORATION.
POSTMASTER: Send address changes to Ideals, Post Office Box 148000, Nashville, Tenn. 37214
All rights reserved. Title IDEALS registered U.S. Patent Office.
Published simultaneously in Canada.

SINGLE ISSUE—$3.50
ONE-YEAR SUBSCRIPTION—eight consecutive issues as published–$15.95
TWO-YEAR SUBSCRIPTION—sixteen consecutive issues as published–$27.95
Outside U.S.A., add $4.00 per subscription year for postage and handling
The cover and entire contents of IDEALS are fully protected by copyright and must not be reproduced in any
manner whatsoever. Printed and bound in U.S.A.
by The Banta Co., Menasha, Wisconsin

Front and back covers by Fred Sieb

Of Loving You

Roses speak of loving you
Their scent a glad refrain
Of all the many years we've spent
Through sunny days and rain.

Roses speak of ways we care
Of fragile things and bright.
Of moonlight walks and silent times
And hands to hold at night.

Roses speak of many things
They hold a special charm.
And sharing them, I sense again
Your hand upon my arm.

Thelma Anna Martin

Country Chronicle

On a February day many winters ago, I first met my Valentine, a blue-eyed southern blonde to whom I had been writing letters for more than eight years.

When our correspondence began, I was thirteen; Lucile was ten. Her aunt had married my older brother. They had met while he was in training in South Carolina, prior to service in France during the first World War. After their marriage, they settled in New York, the ex-soldier's home state. When Lucile wrote her aunt and asked for the name of "some little boy up North" to whom she could write letters, my brother's new wife sent my name.

After I had finished high school and had worked a year on the farm, I decided to take a southern vacation to meet the girl to whom I had been writing. I made the trip in one of Ford's first A models, driving nearly a thousand miles from the cold and snowy countryside of upstate New York to a milder wintertime in the rolling foothills of the Blue Ridge.

I stayed with my sister-in-law's mother, and it was a warm sunny afternoon when Lucile, then a high school senior, stopped in after school to see her grandmother. We met, and I

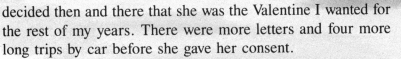

decided then and there that she was the Valentine I wanted for the rest of my years. There were more letters and four more long trips by car before she gave her consent.

Now, after more than half a century of married life, I still consider her my sparkling jewel—wife, lover, and Valentine. Together we have shared the sorrows and cares that come into a long lifetime, but we have also shared the joys and happiness that marriage can bring into flower. The years have mellowed our lives, and blessed them with tenderness, love, and compassion.

In one of my essays in my first book, *A Hill Farm Year,* I wrote of my Valentine in these words:

> She makes more lovely the hours by the tended gardens of bloom that line the walks. Her gentle hands that touch the earth have made the hills more beautiful. The year around she listens with me to the harvest of songs, the warble of the bluebird in March, the summer carillon of the thrush, the autumn orchestra of katydids and crickets, and the song of wind in swirling winter snows.

But perhaps the dedication of the book tells my story better than any other I could hope to write: "To Lucile, whose love of hills brings sun and song into a room."

She and the sun and the song still bless my home and life.

Lansing Christman

FEBRUARY

February can be wild
With her storms of sleet and snow.
Other times she can be mild
With a preview of spring's show.

February's very gay
With St. Valentine to share,
As sweet Cupid on his day
Shoots his arrow through the air.

February's quite a tease
Pulling tricks from out her bag,
Tempting us with springtime's breeze
Like a comic's clever gag.

Then she settles down once more
In her dour mid-winter's role,
Oft appearing at our door
As a poor defenseless soul.

Since her stay is not too long
We must take her in our stride,
Cheering with a merry song
Until days are warm and mild.

Carice Williams

Happy Valentine's Day

February is the month
   When hearts go on display;
In every card shop window
   There's a fanciful array.

Painted hearts and lacy hearts,
   Some with darts and cupid's bow,
And on each card endearing words
   That say, "I love you so."

I'd like to fill the mailman's pack
   Up to the very brim
With valentines to bless each home
   And all who dwell within.

I'd like to make a mother smile
   And brighten Grandma's eyes,
And give a dad who feels left out
   A shiny bright surprise.

I'd like to give to every child
   A valentine to treasure;
One that says "Without a doubt
   You're loved beyond all measure!"

For all the lonely hearts I'd add
   A special line or two,
Letting them know that they are loved
   Each day the whole year through!

A super giant valentine
   To the world I'd send;
I'd ask all nations to join hearts
   And truly be good friends.

I'd fill each mailman's pack sky-high
   With loving hearts entwined,
Until the whole wide world became
   A great big valentine!

                              Kay Hoffman

My Valentine

I found it today in a box put away
With letters faded and brown;
With a fan and a bow from the long ago
A flower and a blue silken gown.

Not a treasure of art. Just a wreath on a heart,
And a verse on a rose-bordered page.
A bit of the past that went by too fast.
A valentine yellowed with age.

With a sigh and a smile, I held it awhile
From the dark of its scented retreat.
Those days were fair—those hours so rare.
The first love of youth is so sweet.

I found it today. Put it gently away,
And remembered the day that it came.
I bent lightly to press one more caress
Where my love had written his name.

Lucille Crumley

February Moment

In winter when the sunset's glow
Spills red across the land of snow,
And skies are painted azure blue,
My heart is filled with warmth anew.

The laden skies—cold and gray—
That sped the snow upon its way
Seem lighter now and fit for spring,
For south-flown birds to come again.

Though March may come with wintry roar
And heap the snow about our door,
This special moment—bright and clear—
Brings hope that spring is very near.

Craig E. Sathoff

Farm Boy's Valentine

Across the moonlit fields I shall be going
To Miller's pond, where young folks meet to skate.
And with me, gay in scarlet tam and sweater,
Arm linked with mine, in way affectionate,
My bonnie brown-eyed, brown-haired, gladsome Mary
This bracing zero day in February.

Across the rimy, withered fields of stubble
Where, here and there, the snow lies drifted still.
Across the stile I used to help her over
When walking to the schoolhouse on the hill.
On rainy days we shared the same umbrella
And I was always known as "Mary's fellow."

May Allread Baker

Maker of Songs

He made the little songs that people love,
Heart-clutching little songs, of homely things,
That bring a tender laughter to the eyes,
A sadness, that is like the brush of wings:

He sang of quaint wee maids in pinafores,
    And red geraniums on a window sill,
Of curtains edged in snowy ruffled scrim,
    And lullabies, when tiny feet are still.

He sang of soft warm arms that hold one close,
    And trim white cottages, with garden plots
Of mellow loam, and rows of jade-green peas,
    Of woodsy byways, and forget-me-nots.

He never sang the busy world he knew—
    The restless turmoil of the mill, and mart—
A world that had denied these humbler joys.
    He sang the hunger that was in his heart.

Jessie Wilmore Murton

Overleaf
ON A WINTER'S DAY
Three Lions

Photo Opposite
LOVE'S OLD SWEET SONG
H. Armstrong Roberts

Readers' Reflections

My Heart Is Yours

I have two arms to give to you
To hold you and caress,
To do my best to bring to you
A bit of happiness.

I have two lips to speak soft words
So meaningful and true,
To tell you what it means to me
To share my life with you.

I only have one heart to give
But it is yours, my dear,
For you make life a paradise
Whenever you are near.

Carice Williams
Riverside, Illinois

Editor's Note: Readers are invited to submit poetry, short anecdotes, and humorous reflections on life for possible publication in future *Ideals* issues. Please send copies only; manuscripts will not be returned. Writers will receive $10 for each published submission. Send materials to "Readers' Reflections," Ideals Publishing Corporation, Nelson Place at Elm Hill Pike, Nashville, Tennessee 37214.

Colors of Love

Imagine a rainbow
    Of black and white,
A moonless sky
    On a starless night...

Picture a sunrise,
    A colorless sun,
Pale autumn leaves
    When summer's done...

Envision a garden
    Dreary and gray,
Lackluster roses in
    A bridal bouquet...

Now faded and dismal
    God's earth would be
Without any colors
    For our eyes to see!

He paints us a rainbow
    After each storm,
Flowers in springtime
    When earth is warm...

And there on his canvas
    In heaven above,
He paints every sunrise
    With colors of love!

Clay Harrison
Tampa, Florida

Love Is

It's older than this age-old world,
It's deeper than the sea,
It's richer than the purest gold...
'Twill live eternally.

It comes in many colors,
Has seen both joy and pain;
It thrives in fertile soil...
Endures both sun and rain.

It needs no wrapping paper,
This gift so fine and rare;
It is the gift of pure sweet love...
It's the spoken words, "I care."

Love is all of this and more;
Its length and depth unknown,
And when it's freely given...
It's a gift that stands alone.

Marie A. Florian
Eaton Rapids, Michigan

Music-Box Valentine

So delicate and full of charm
With figurines that, arm in arm,
Gracefully whirl themselves around
To an enchanting, tinkling sound.

What pleasant hours I spend with you,
Reminder of one's love so true.
Little music box of mine,
You're a very special valentine.

Nadine Brothers Lybarger
Owasso, Oklahoma

Valentines

It's fun remembering days gone by,
The valentines that made us sigh,
The box at school with bright red hearts
That held the penny cards with darts
Or homemade greetings made in haste
With lacey trims and flour paste.

How we loved each valentine
With sentiment, "Will you be mine?"
These gems now rest in faded books,
Tucked away in storage nooks.
It's great when there is time to while
To read again these cards and smile.

We reminisce about those days
So much a part of memory's maze,
And wonder 'bout the friends of yore,
Who added to our childhood lore;
Those whose names are on the lines
Of our keepsake valentines!

Virginia Borman Grimmer
Schererville, Indiana

A Buggy Adventure

I must relate the story
About the Sunday ride
With Mr. Charles Landley
In the buggy at my side.

We were trotting very gently
Along the elm-lined lanes,
When Mr. Landley asked if
I might like to take the reins.

We were cantering so calmly
Along the country road
When Mr. Landley, mercy me,
Began to get quite bold!

He placed his hand upon my arm
And began to talk such nonsense.
Why, with both my hands engaged,
I found myself defenseless!

I set that buggy on a course
For home at such a rate,
That Mr. Landley was astounded
When we halted at the gate.

It must have been Charles' kiss
That set my senses astray,
Or else I would not have said "yes"
To a ride again next Sunday!

Cornell M. Brellenthin

Special Delivery

In London days so long ago,
Behind a front of dignity,
Lovers knew delightful ways
To carry on in secrecy.

A lady's fan upon her cheek
A lilac-scented letter
Could tell a man that o'er the rest,
She thought he was much better.

Yet, no young lover's language
Could convey a whole rorhance
Quite as sweetly and completely
As the London postage stamp.

If a lady was well-bred
And sought a man with proper grace
She could send a proper message
Stamped in the proper place.

With a stamp placed to the right
On an envelope she'd send
A message to her heart's desire,
"I want to be your friend."

If a man was not quite ready,
Didn't want to settle down,
He'd return the lady's message
With a stamp placed upside down.

The lady knew, of course,
That "Write no more" was what he meant,
But a very persistent lady
Flipped a stamp and placed it left.

Any gentleman was flattered
With that message, "I love you,"
But stamping left-hand corner
He'd sweetly bid "Adieu."

When a lady's heart was broken,
She found it could be mended
With "Accept my love," stamped lower right,
From a new love who had sent it.

And if, by any chance, in time,
Her former love came 'round,
He'd send a letter with a stamp,
Placed sideways, right, and down.

He meant "I long to see you."
But alas, the lady jilted
Promptly stamped another letter
On the left and slightly tilted.

Any knowledgeable man,
By a cock-eyed stamp was shaken.
He knew he'd waited far too long,
The lady's heart was taken.

It seems the London postmen
Grew weary of this game,
For they now require everyone
To place their stamps the same.

But you can rest assured
That young love will find new ways,
Of winning hearts and breaking hearts
As they did in olden days.

D. L. Cornell

When the Moon Is a Silver Canoe

When the moon is a silver canoe,
I'll go sailing along with you
Down the river of dreams,
Chasing silver moonbeams,
'Til the sun gathers diamonds of dew.

True love is a wonderful thing;
In our hearts, it's eternally spring.
Side by side, Dear, with you,
Our dreams will come true
When the moon is a silver canoe.

Dorothy M. Goerke

Frances Carter Yost

Frances Carter Yost was born in View, Idaho, and educated in Utah. Although she considered her writing to be a hobby, she could not remember a time when she did not want to write. She wrote in her journal: "It is hard to express on paper the part writing has played in my life. Because it is such a part of my life that I cannot separate it from myself, I truly believe that I was born with the urge."

Mrs. Yost loved being with people who shared her love of writing, and was a member of the Utah Poetry Society and the Idaho Press Women. She was a correspondent and columnist for ten newspapers, and her stories and articles appeared in several magazines. She published two books of poetry, *Brim With Joy* and *While Orchids Bloom,* and was the editor of *Bancroft's Book of Remembrance* and *Missionary Memoirs.* Several of her poems have appeared in *Ideals,* and these are a selection from her book *While Orchids Bloom.*

Miniature Garden

In the garden of your heart,
Of your heart's desire
You have locked the gems to which
Bravely I aspire.
Joys of life and love to share,
These you lock in keeping.
Have you thrown the key away,
Torn my heart with weeping?
Though the moons fail, I shall wait
Patient at your garden gate.

Miniature Memories

Here is but a scrap of cloth,
Scrap of calico.
Dress from it is thread-bare now.
Worn out long ago.
Bluebells on a yellow field,
Butterflies a tilting,
I was proud to wear that frock
Set my heart a lilting.
Strange! the pictures that I see,
Scrapbags hold a memory.

Miniature Man

Watch him as he goes to work,
Goes in overalls,
With shirt opened at the neck,
"Bye Bye Mom," he calls.
Armed with hammer, nails and saw
Glad notes he is trilling.
While he builds a house or barn
My own heart is thrilling.
He looks up; his blue eyes shine
Three years old; and he is mine.

The Welcome Mat

Kitty dozing at the door,
At the entranceway,
Tells that friendly folks live here,
Beckons one to stay.
Speaks of love and fireside glow,
Peacefully lies sleeping.
Mother never scoots her off
As she does her sweeping.
Why not lift our knocker too?
Friendly folks will welcome you!

Nosegays for Sale!

Violets with heart-shaped leaves,
Hearts that touch the earth—
I picked two large baskets' full—
Such a wealth of dearth.
I have snipped since morning light
Little passion posy.
Soft with dew and shyly coy,
Nosegays are so cozy.
Father: soften hearts today
Help me sell each wee bouquet.

A Flower Garden Cake

I watched the Mrs. make a cake
With flour, eggs and spice.
She mixed and poured it in to bake
What fragrance to entice.

I shall mix my recipe too.
Ingredients of art.
Forsythia along the fence
Four bushes for a start.

I plant arabis, thriving plant
Which creeps around for show,
Then stir in shoals of daffodils
Chaste white, pale golds that glow.

For spice I add a small spring bulb
Siberica of blue
A dash of chinodoza roots (keen-o-doxa)
I place in warm soil too.

They bake all winter in the ground
Beneath the snow's caress.
Spring flings her wand and you will see
A cake of loveliness!

A Toast to the Bride

Here's to the bride: May she be gay
And happy as she is today.
    Have health, success, a nursery,
    A handsome husband's courtesy,
Blue skies, some wealth, and time to play.

Life is a song, a symphony.
And marriage is the melody.
    Trials are tempos which lend sway.
    Here's to the bride.

Now this advice may I convey.
The worth of it, I hope you weigh.
    In little things use liberty,
    In big things use philosophy,
        To make your life a roundelay.
        Here's to the bride!

Overleaf
OLD-FASHIONED NOSEGAY
H. Armstrong Roberts

Candyland and Flowers

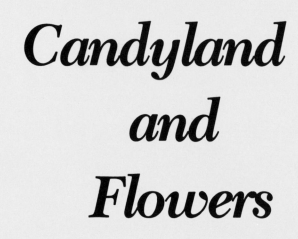

Candyland and flowers,
Lollipops and creams,
Lilies of the valley,
Honeysuckle dreams.

Ice cream, cake and lilacs,
Peppermint so fine,
Dandelion memories—
All of this is mine.

Sugar-coated kisses,
Orange blossom smile,
Licorice love forever,
Candy kind of style.

Chocolate-covered daydreams,
Roses with their dew,
Rhymes and maple syrup—
It's all because of you.

Lemonade and cookies,
Daisies and a song,
Bubblegum and tulips,
Nothing can go wrong.

Violets and cheesecake,
The daffodils are ours.
Our love is just a world of
Candyland and flowers.

Tamara Schoonover

Loves Me...
Loves Me Not

When e'er I see a daisy,
I am mindful of the time,
When I plucked the petals,
To the old familiar rhyme.

For it was a childhood custom,
And a sentimental chance,
To discover which fair maiden
Would be partial to romance.

I recall my tense elation,
As I drew the last one out,
For the rhyme and final petal,
Meant I'd won without a doubt.

John Fenton Lowry

Say It with Flowers

Expressions of love are often poetic, frequently musical, and even occasionally dramatic. Yet what words can compare with the silent eloquence of one perfect flower? Perhaps this is the reason the ancients wove a rich tapestry of myth, legend and folklore around flowers, endowing each bloom with special meaning. A bouquet could speak of undying devotion or of a broken heart. It is a language meant for lovers and one lovers ought to learn.

As children, we played "loves-me, loves-me-not" with the petals of a daisy. When the last petal and phrase revealed the outcome, it was child-like faith that claimed the prophecy true. How fitting, then, that innocence is the daisy's message. It conveys the still-bright hopes of a youthful heart.

Another blossom linked with first love is the fragrant lilac. Its delicate lavender color was thought to speak of melancholy, however, and a gift of lilacs often indicated the ending of an engagement. Many a hesitant lover allowed the purple clusters to reveal what words could not.

While the lilac speaks of broken vows, the rose has long implied the opposite. Roman legend claims the rose first became red when Venus pricked her fingers on the thorny stems and crimson drops of blood fell on the pure white blooms. Having thus received its color from the goddess of love, it is understandable that the rose has historically spoken of true devotion and fidelity.

The fragile violet also traces its meaning to ancient mythology. It is said that Cupid was called upon to settle a dispute between Venus and a group of beautiful maidens. In this mythical beauty contest, Cupid declared the maidens more lovely. Seized with a jealous rage, Venus beat the unfortunate girls until they were blue, whereupon they were magically transformed into the first violets. Because of this, the violet is linked with the image of modesty and humility, a small purple reminder of hidden loveliness.

Even more poignant is the story of the forget-me-not, a symbol of enduring love. The legend is that as a pair of young lovers strolled beside the Danube, the maid spied a cluster of lovely blossoms on the opposite bank. To please her, the young man plunged into the river, swam across and retrieved the blooms. On his return, however, a huge wave bore him away. As he was swept out to sea, he threw the bouquet to his beloved, calling, "Forget me not!" With such romantic beginnings, it is understandable that this delicate blue flower has come to signify love and remembrance in the language of the flowers.

With or without elaborate histories, all kinds of flowers are endowed with special meanings, useful in sending a message of love. Consider the following: Do you experience great temptation from the object of your affection? A branch of apple blossoms will convey your plight. Is there a secret, untold love you'd like to reveal? The heady sweet perfume of the waxy gardenia will relay your message. Even the lowly dandelion becomes a courier of love when its fluffy seeds are blown to carry thoughts to your beloved.

Perhaps the meanings of these flowers appear too subtle. In that case, the tulip might be more appropriate. A Persian poet wrote: "As the redness of this flower, I am on fire with love; as the blackness of its center, my heart is burnt to a coal with desire." Now there's a flower that speaks volumes!

Whether one is an impassioned poet or a retiring secret admirer, there is little to match the eloquence expressed by the unspoken promise of petal and perfume. In the language of love, perhaps there is an advantage in learning to say it with flowers.

Pamela Kennedy

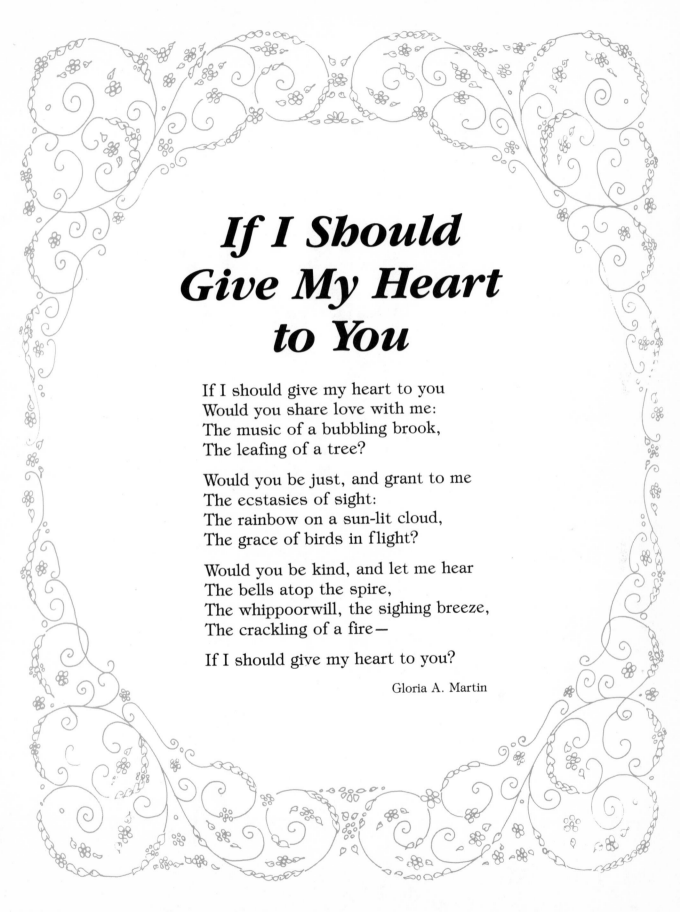

If I Should Give My Heart to You

If I should give my heart to you
Would you share love with me:
The music of a bubbling brook,
The leafing of a tree?

Would you be just, and grant to me
The ecstasies of sight:
The rainbow on a sun-lit cloud,
The grace of birds in flight?

Would you be kind, and let me hear
The bells atop the spire,
The whippoorwill, the sighing breeze,
The crackling of a fire—

If I should give my heart to you?

Gloria A. Martin

The Sky, the Moon, the Stars

Do you remember once at twilight
When the sky was a clear blue,
The grass a velvet green, I called to you
To come and see the new young moon?

You took my hand and we stood still
For we had never seen so rare a sight,
Jupiter, brilliant-bright,
Was set upon that golden crescent's point.

Remember how it looked?
Just like a jeweled pin set in the evening blue;
A star below it hung like a drop of dew
Catching its brilliance from some hidden light.

The blue grew deeper as we watched,
The red-gold planets and the moon
More and more radiant, soon
They lost their sweet, ethereal light.

But we shall never lose the lovely picture that they made,
The sky, the moon, the evening stars,
It is forever ours
To treasure on into the night.

Alice B. Dorland

Strawberry Bavarian Sponge Torte

2 3-ounce packages strawberry gelatin
1 cup boiling water
2 packages frozen sliced strawberries,
slightly thawed
½ pint heavy cream, whipped
(or whipped topping)
1 sponge cake, cut in cubes
Whipped cream to decorate
Fresh berries to decorate

Dissolve gelatin in boiling water. Add berries and allow to partially thicken. Fold in ½ pint whipped cream. Toss with cake cubes and place in a greased springform or large mixing bowl. Chill torte overnight. Turn out on platter and frost with whipped cream. Garnish with whole strawberries. Serves 10 to 12.

Love Tokens

For centuries gloves have been a popular present to give to one's Valentine on the 14th of February; the custom goes back at least to the 16th century. Expensive gifts in the form of jewelry were usual among the wealthier and more exalted; no doubt ordinary folk gave gifts of jewels and trinkets, too, but accounts and records of those in more humble stations of life have not been handed down in the same way.

From the diary of Samuel Pepys we learn that garters were also commonly given to one's Valentine, and we hear of little Will Mercer making a prettily ornamented card with a name designed on it.

An interesting love token from about 1700 is a traditional design of a heart which measures about an inch and a half across and is covered with a rich brocade in red and white on one side and entirely in red on the other. The little metal arrow which pierces it is tipped with chicken's feathers.

Sailors thought fondly of their sweethearts while away on their long voyages, and spent the time by carving or scratching designs on pieces of tusk or bone. These drawings, known as scrimshaw work, are sometimes most attractively done. Often they show a ship, or a scene at sea, and carry loving and affectionate messages. Common gifts of this kind were stay busks, which were stiffeners for corsets. One of these stay busks was carved out of a hard wood: the upper end is adorned by a heart, while in the lower part can be seen the traditional pair of doves. A portrait in the middle might well be that of the giver. On the other side is carved the date, and the lady's name. An even more elaborate reminder of this sort of token is the busk carved from a sperm whale's jaw and having the lines:

> Accept, dear girl, this busk from me
> Carved by my humble hand
> I took it from a sperm whale's jaw
> One thousand miles from land.
> In many a gale Had been the whale
> In which this bone did rest
> His time is past, His bone at last
> Must now support thy breast.

Love tokens, too, were commonly little ivory or bone bobbins used for making lace. Love messages delicately pricked in along the sides would say "The gift is small

but love is all," or "My love for thee no one can tell," and other simple expressions of this sort.

Another kind of love token mostly favored in country districts was the knitting sheath, which was a piece of wood about 9 inches long, decoratively carved to the best of the giver's ability. Having a hole at one end, it was fashioned in such a way that, when tucked into a waist belt, the wearer would have her right hand free.

In the latter part of the 18th century it would be common for a young woman to give her sweetheart a small circular piece of material of silk or satin, the size of a watch, on which she had embroidered her name, with the date and an expression of affection such as "Remember Me," or her initials along with those of her lover enclosed in a heart. These were used instead of the ordinary watch papers which, embellished with fine engraving and the name of the watchmaker, were commonly put inside the enveloping metal case of a watch, and served to keep the dust out of the works.

The handmade True-Love Knots, the puzzle purses, and other decorative handwritten letters with sets of verses and sentimental messages of love were the forerunners of the pictorial valentine as we know it today. Along with these, in the early years of the 19th century and up to the 1850s, little containers and comfit boxes of Bilston or Battersea ware were inscribed with a well-chosen sentiment.

Mugs, cups, jugs and dishes of Sunderland ware made useful valentines. One example of these is a handsome jug of Liverpool ware decorated like a valentine; the Endless Knot of Love is on one side, and a picture on the other.

A most delightful love token is a neatly bound little volume of love poems; the edges of the pages are gilded, but fore-edged, so that by slightly fanning out the pages a colored design is revealed with the words: "To My Valentine."

It follows, of course, that love tokens were given on any occasion and at any time, and not only on the 14th of February, although St. Valentine's Day was often favored.

Today some people may think of valentines only as lovely lace-edged pictorial cards with verses. However, a valentine does not need to be a pretty picture with verses, and for centuries past a gift to one's sweetheart in the form of gloves, garters, jewelry—anything, in fact, given with love—was accepted by way of a valentine gift.

Frank Staff

A China Plate

She gave a cherished little dish
Kept forty years with pride
To her young niece, soon to become,
As she was once, a bride.

Because she loved it very much,
Its happy years and days
Will be renewed and added to,
Instead of laid away.

This is the pattern of her life,
And this treasure from her shelf
Will carry memories of love
Transplanted from herself.

Dan A. Hoover

The Flower Wedding

When young **Sweet William aster**
If she would be his bride,
Miss **Black-eyed Susan** answered "yes"
And swayed close to his side.

Beneath her lovely wedding gown
Of dainty **Queen Anne's lace**,
She wore a satin **cowslip** that
Clung to her form with grace.

She wore **foxgloves** upon her hands,
Coxcombs held her hair,
Lady-slippers sheathed her feet—
They made a bonny pair.

The **Canterbury bells** rang out
To wish them joy through life
As **Jack-in-the-pulpit** said the words
That made them man and wife.

Her mother had to **balsam** for
She found it all confusing—
Her **bleeding heart** was bruised and sore,
A daughter she was losing.

The **dogwood** barked and scared the groom,
The **dandelions** roared!
Snapdragons frightened all the guests
Until peace was restored.

Soon after they were wed she cut
His **batchelor buttons** off,
And he foreswore his **Indian pipe**
Because it made her cough.

He gave her gifts of **candytuft**,
Bought with his **marigold**,
And purchased **Johnny-jump-up** toys
When his first **phlox** were sold.

The **milkweed** furnished all their milk,
The **four-o'clock** told time;
They worshipped every **baby's breath**—
Their marriage was sublime!

Emily Carey Alleman

Overleaf
WITH THIS RING
Robert Barclay
Grant Heilman Photography

Tender Conscience

We were puttering, cleaning out drawers, the cedar
chest…taking out things, replacing them…
souvenirs of our lives:

Why do I cling to some old thing
Which no one would admire.
Why reminisce and see the bliss
In a thing that lost its fire…

An empty box, which had held a ring,
And the music to make my heart sing.
White satin dress with gloves and shoes to match,
Dried-up bouquet which the girls did not catch.

A pinafore, the very first I wore...
It couldn't compete with the least in a store.
Little white box that is falling apart...
Four tiny booties which I hold to my heart...
The girl's and the boy's, old, wrinkled and gray,
But I remember their steps to the day.

Rattles and marbles...my first birthday gift,
Handmade by love, how it gave me a lift!
Diplomas and honors...the growing up,
Climbing the ladder with grades to the top.
And then, I find a folded-up note,
Tenderness speaks in the few words he wrote.

I sort and sort, and neatly place it back.
There's nothing here which, in value, seems to lack.

I reminisce through all this
Nothing is cast aside.
Time is not spent as it has lent
Gems of the mother, sweetheart and bride.

Helen Nencka

Come Indoors

Come indoors and rest a spell,
Get acquainted with yourself.
Toast your shins at an open hearth,
Take a book down from the shelf.
Follow where the author leads,
Read of brave and valiant deeds.

Come indoors while fields lie deep
Underneath a foot of snow.
Shut your eyes and travel far
With daring tales of long ago.
Visit lands you've never seen,
Countries always warm and green.

Come indoors, get out your tools,
Mend a shelf or fix a door,
Tinker with a broken lock,
Smooth a rough place on the floor.
In the doing you will find
Happiness and peace of mind.

Underneath your own brown roof
Is a wealth of joy unguessed.
Happiness of family ties,
All the dearest and the best.
Come indoors, where you can claim
All of these in love's dear name.

Edna Jaques

Photo Opposite
RED HOUSE IN WINTER
Fred Sieb

The Golden Afternoon

I took my little braided rug
And laid it by my fire;
I drew two chairs beside the hearth
And piled the dry wood higher;

The kettle started singing out,
The cat began her purring,
No other sound was in the room
Except the small clock's whirring.

It struck the hour and then was still,
The room was sweet and quiet;
I was so glad my fire burned
And I was sitting by it;

I was so glad the sun shone in,
And that I had one flower;
A little scarlet spray of light
To brighten that good hour.

The other chair was empty quite,
No one came in—and only
The kettle, cat, and I were there
But still I was not lonely.

My mind ran bright with happiness
As glowing as an ember...
Strange, how the heart will choose one hour
From many, to remember!

Grace Noll Crowell

A Discovery

I had the most wonderful time today
With the world at my fingertips,
The globe on my desk was spinning away
Inviting gay, make-believe trips.

Skimming the ocean and islands and seas,
I hopscotched to England and France,
Floating to Spain on a westerly breeze
I touched upon Italy by chance;

And I would have tarried longer in Rome
But a strange thing happened to me:
Mountains and rivers and cities of home
Were suddenly things I must "see."

Quick as a wink I was back in my chair
And looking around with "new" eyes
It seemed that my room was waiting to share
A wealth of delightful surprise.

A bright colored globe, still spinning around,
And my book of geography
Are always filled with adventure, I found
If only you want them to be!

Viney Wilder Endicott

A Boy
with
a Book

A boy with a book on a winter night,
Reading the stories by firelight—
Pilgrim's Progress and Aesop's lore,
Washington's courage in peace and war;

Stretching out flat in a shady nook
When summertime came, with a treasured book;
Or perching with ease on a fence rail stout,
Spelling Old Testament stories out;

Filling his soul with the heritage
All boys may find in the printed page,
Learning the lessons that patriots know—
Young Abe Lincoln of long ago.

Margaret Oleson

Rachel and Andrew: Love Above Scandal

e've got to get to the top, Rachel, then no one will be able to climb high enough to attack us," said Andrew Jackson at a time when slander and gossip about the two of them were at a peak of frenzy. Andrew reached that pinnacle when he was elected president of the United States, but Rachel, his beloved wife, was never to share his success as his first lady.

As a girl, Rachel Donelson went with her father to the Tennessee frontier where she was the finest dancer and horsewoman of that young state. In her generation men drank whiskey from a barrel, and girls and women smoked pipes, dipped snuff, and wore homespun dresses and sunbonnets. Yet the moral code of the leaders of frontier society was strict, and Rachel came from a prominent Tennessee family.

Shortly after Rachel married her first husband, a young Revolutionary War hero named Mr. Robards, she realized that although handsome and romantic, he was moody, possessive, quick-tempered, and unreasonably jealous. She was patient and forgiving when he drank, and she tried to smooth over quarrels, but she could not condone his infidelity with a servant. Separation or divorce was unknown in that era, and was a disgrace. It took a lot of courage for Rachel to return to her mother's home.

Andrew Jackson, a young lawyer, met Rachel while boarding with her family. They had a great deal in common and their romance ignited like wildfire. Aware of this, Rachel's husband threatened and actually instituted a divorce suit in order to cover up his own actions and embarrass both Rachel and An-

drew. He named Jackson as respondent and labeled Rachel an adultress.

However, the resulting stigma was not sufficient to destroy the love of Rachel and Andrew, and they married in the belief that Rachel's former husband had secured a divorce. Upon learning he had not done so, Jackson obtained Rachel's divorce and they remarried. The Jacksons had no children, although they did adopt her sister's son who was renamed Andrew Jackson, Jr., and who later inherited the president's estates.

Andrew Jackson was the "hope of the common people" of his generation. Born in South Carolina, he was a boy when war raged between the American colonies and the British. Both his parents died when he was a child, and his two older brothers died in prison during the Revolutionary War. Without kin to guide or help him, Andrew was determined to build his own future and make the world recognize him. He learned to care for himself as one who is a leader among men must do.

Rachel was an ideal woman for Jackson. She was a striking figure in his early career, and during their marriage he felt that there was nothing too good for her. They were happy at the Hermitage (their home) until General Jackson became president. She died the December before his inauguration, and was buried in the white satin gown she was to have worn to the Inaugural Ball. Although cherished by her husband, she had been haunted by the disgrace she had suffered. When she was notified that her husband had won the election she told his manager, "For Mr. Jackson's sake, I am glad. For my

own part, I never wished it."

Upon Rachel's death, her niece Emily (whose husband, Major Andrew J. Donelson, was Jackson's private secretary) assumed the role left unfilled by Rachel. Emily had innate refinement, grace, and dignity which added much to the brilliancy of this noted era. Her four children were born in the White House. During the last year of Jackson's second term, Emily's health failed. She developed consumption and died in December of the same year.

Emily was an admirable first lady, but Jackson never forgot his beloved Rachel. In his many letters to his adopted son, Jackson wrote, "You have been reared in the paths of virtue and morality by a pious and amiable mother....since I have been deprived of your dear mother there is no happiness or contentment for me on this side of the grave....the only object that makes life desirable to me is to see you happy, prosperous and settled in life." Rachel and Andrew had shared forty years of love, and Jackson honored his devoted wife with this epitaph: "A being so gentle, and yet so virtuous, slander might wound, but could not dishonor."

Gertrude Zeth Brooks

The Raggedy Dolls Speak

Raggedy Ann looked a little sad
And her candy heart was, too,
As she gazed at Andy, old and worn
With his blue hat quite askew.

"Your arm needs fixing again, I see!
And your mouth has had too much kissing!
That shirt is so very faded
And another button missing!"

"Your apron is not so snowy white.
Your curls of yarn seem to sag.
Just look at the dust on this tea set.
I don't think that you can brag!"

"We've been packed away for quite a while.
You may think it a little sad.
I do, too, until I recall
The fun and the joy we had!"

Barbara Moran

Photo Opposite
RAG DOLLS
Gary Blodgett

Story Hour

When I was just a little girl
I'd climb on Daddy's knee
Most every Sunday afternoon
While he would read to me.

He'd tell each story from my book
In words I understood
And helped me to enjoy my books
The way he thought I should.

And from these precious story hours
When Daddy read to me
A love for books grew in my heart
That's lasted constantly.

Today I do not dream and yearn
For things I do not need
I'm happy with my lot in life
And favorite books to read.

Carice Williams

A Friendly Book

A winter's day, a glowing fire
A warm and cozy nook,
When hearts find true companionship
Within a friendly book.

To strange far lands you may travel,
Or quiet countryside,
As enchanting doors of dreamland
Swing open for you wide.

The glowing fire, the friendly book,
Memories to treasure,
As time stands still and sweet content
Fills your heart with pleasure.

Vera Hardman

Needlepoint

Stitching with colored threads
Helps me pass the hours.
It keeps my fingers busy
With colors bright as flowers.
It keeps my memory busy
Which makes this pastime fun,
And brings to mind old pictures
Of playing in the sun.

"Green" brings back our picnics
Spread out on the grass,
"Blues," the rivers, brooks, and ocean,
As fleecy "white" clouds pass.
"Red" the cheeks of sturdy babes—
We've cuddled quite a few.
"Yellow" curls match my wool,
How fast the growth years flew!

And now I do my needlepoint
But people never know
How I relive in colored thread
The days of long ago.

Helen Heberer

Photo Opposite
NEEDLEWORK
Barry Runk
Grant Heilman Photography

To Each His Own

Time was when I was loath to say
I never learned to sew,
When asked by one who knew which way
Each stitch and seam should go;

And several times I truly tried
To master this great art
With patterns more than simplified,
But always I lost heart.

Now I've learned it's much more wise
To really be content
With making tasty apple pies
For which my hands were meant.

This little lesson carries through
As you have surely guessed,
There's something each of us can do
Not merely good but best;

So if your talent runs to pies,
Just use it, don't apologize!

Viney Wilder Endicott

Homemade Bread

She took a bit of leaven,
Then added lots of flour;
Stirred in salt and sugar,
And let it stand an hour.

Then she took the soft dough
And shaped it with her hand;
She put it in a warm place
So the mixture could expand.

She popped it in the oven
To bake a little while;
Out came golden loaves
That would make the hungry smile.

Very few ingredients
And even fewer tools,
A little bit of hard work;
Observing certain rules.

'Twas such a simple method
To let her family know
How much she really loved them—
Her warm bread told them so.

Marie A. Florian

A Winter Sunday

I love a peaceful Sunday,
The quiet that's in the air,
The serene and happy feeling,
The comfortable rocking chair.

The smell of delicious coffee,
The ham and hot cakes to bake.
No hurried school-day rushing,
No scampering, no lunches to make.

The papers piled high on the table,
You can read to your heart's delight
With an old soft robe and slippers on
And the sun shining warm and bright.

I love a quiet Sunday
With peacefulness in the air.
Let's count our blessings, go to church,
And say a little prayer.

Marguerite Halker

Contentment

Evening nearing–
   Day is drawing to an end.
Time endearing–
   In family closeness evening spend.

   Firelight flickering–
      Shadows moving on the wall.
   Music playing–
      Pleasant warmth stirs through us all.

      Perfect ending–
         To a perfect, lovely day.
      Memories gathering–
         That within our hearts will stay.

Janet Kay Wimsett

At Evening

The road winds on into the deepening dusk,
Above the winter sky is soft and gray;
On either side, outlined against the snow,
The forest trees loom dark beside the way.

Before me through the twilight gloom I see
A slender church spire, tall and gleaming white;
A bird skims lightly on its homeward way,
A solemn hush awaits the coming night.

I walk alone within this solitude
And peace of mind and deep content are mine—
Around the wooded curve that lies ahead
I know that I shall see the home lights shine.

Jane Shoemaker

Song of the Sea Children

How unutterably lonely
Is the vast grey round of sea,
Till the yellow flower of heaven
Breaks and blossoms and gets free,
Lighting up the lilac spaces
With her golden density!
Hope of sailors and of lovers,
Swings the lantern of the sea.

Not the moon it was that lighted
One grey waste of heart I know,
Warmed with loving, touched with magic,
And made molten and aglow,
When your beauty flowered above it
From a twilight soft and slow.
Dearest face that still must beacon
Where your lover still must go!

Bliss Carman

Photo Opposite
PORTLAND HEAD LIGHT
Dick Smith

Old Sweethearts

Night after night in the evenings
There by the fire they sit,
Quiet and still in their mem'ries
While lights are dimly lit,
Dreaming of yesterday's gladness
Fond of the hopes they've shared,
Finding the peace of contentment
Proud that they both have cared.

Words are not needed between them
Only a smile and a kiss,
Their love is sure as tomorrow
Filled with a wedded bliss,
Kindness and real understanding
Never a doubt or a fear,
All that they need is each other
All that they hold most dear.

Night after night you will find them
Right in the same old place,
He, with his gentle expression,
She, with her smiling face,
The oldest and dearest of sweethearts
Going through life hand in hand,
Reaping a beautiful harvest
From dreams that they carefully planned.

Garnett Ann Schultz

Overleaf
SHARING A SUNSET
H. Armstrong Roberts

Winter in the Garden

All that can be witnessed from my window as
   I toil
Is a white but rumpled blanket on the rose bed's
   nurturing soil
And a pine tree and a cedar which in green are
   gleaming still,
And some hardy, hungry sparrows on my narrow
   window sill.

Like a bed the boy has slept in now the ground
   appears to be,
With the blankets piled and twisted, scarcely fit for
   folks to see;
With the things he has discarded, helter-skelter
   strewn about—
Thus the garden strikes my fancy every time that
   I look out.

There's a curious sort of calmness over shrub and
   plant and vine,
And the sleeping trees stand solemn as the winds
   about them whine.
Now the song birds have departed and the loneliness
   and gloom
Give the earth a curious likeness to a boy's deserted
   room.

Edgar A. Guest

It's Easter at Ideals!

Come join us as we herald the arrival of spring and the Easter season in Easter Ideals, our next issue. Share with us beautiful photographs of the first flowers of spring, and the joyous celebrations of Easter. Take a walk with us through a modern Garden of Eden. Find out how other countries use eggs in celebrations of Easter. Remember with us Easters past and present, especially the wondrous promise of the first Easter morning.

Join us, and share the celebration with others. A gift subscription is an excellent way to bring the beauty and wonder of spring to a friend.

Statement of ownership, management and circulation (Required by 39 U.S.C. 3685), of IDEALS, published 8 times a year in Feb.; Mar.; May; June; Aug.; Sept.; Nov.; Dec. at Nashville, Tennessee, for September 1985. Publisher, Ideals Publishing Corporation; Editor, Ramona Richards; Managing Editor, Ideals Publishing Corporation; Owner, Thomas Nelson, Inc., Nelson Place at Elm Hill Pike, P.O. Box 141000, Nashville, Tennessee 37214. The known bondholders, mortgagees, and other security holders owning or holding 1 percent or more of total amount of bonds, mortgages or other securities are: None. Average no. copies each issue during preceding 12 months: Total no. copies printed (Net Press Run) 241,971. Paid circulation 58,158. Mail subscription 178,413. Total paid circulation 236,571. Free distribution 56. Total distribution 236,627. Actual no. copies of single issue published nearest to filing date: Total no. copies printed (Net Press Run) 187,180. Paid circulation 8,263. Mail subscription 164,447. Total paid circulation 172,710. Free distribution 38. Total distribution 172,748. I certify that the statements made by me above are correct and complete. Patricia A. Pingry, Publisher.

ACKNOWLEDGEMENTS

THE GOLDEN AFTERNOON from *THIS GOLDEN SUMMIT* by Grace Noll Crowell. Copyright 1937 by Harper & Brothers. Used with permission from Harper & Row Publishers, Inc., San Francisco. THE FLOWER WEDDING from *THE GYPSY HEART*, copyright 1957 by Emily Carey Alleman; OLD SWEETHEARTS by Garnett Ann Schultz used by permission of the author from her book *THE LITTLE THINGS*. Our sincere thanks to the following authors whose addresses we were unable to locate: May Allread Baker for FARM BOY'S VALENTINE from her book *WILLOW BROOK FARM*; Gertrude Zeth Brooks for RACHEL AND ANDREW—A GREAT LOVE AFFAIR from the book *FIRST LADIES OF THE WHITE HOUSE* by Gertrude Zeth Brooks, Jan Pitts, Editor, copyright 1969 by Gertrude Zeth Brooks; Mrs. Edward A. Knowles for THE SKY, THE MOON, THE STARS by Alice B. Dorland from the book *ROAMING THE WIND* by Alice B. Dorland; Christopher Thomas Haley for SWEETHEART DAYS; Mrs. Marguerite Halker for A WINTER SUNDAY; Mrs. Helen Heberer for NEEDLEPOINT; John Fenton Lowry for LOVES ME . . . LOVES ME NOT; Gloria A. Martin for IF I SHOULD GIVE MY HEART TO YOU from her book *VELVET PILLOWS OF PERFUME*, copyright 1971 by Gloria A. Martin; Barbara Moran for THE RAGGEDY DOLLS SPEAK; Margaret Oleson for A BOY WITH A BOOK; and Tamara Schoonover for CANDYLAND AND FLOWERS.